To Aidan & Margot,
From my Heart
to yours

ISBN 979-8-88644-959-4 (Paperback)
ISBN 979-8-88644-961-7 (Hardcover)
ISBN 979-8-88644-960-0 (Digital)

Copyright © 2023 Nermine Khouzam Rubin and Susan Joy Bellavance
All rights reserved
First Edition

All rights reserved. No part of this publication may be reproduced, distributed, or transmitted in any form or by any means, including photocopying, recording, or other electronic or mechanical methods without the prior written permission of the publisher. For permission requests, solicit the publisher via the address below.

Covenant Books
11661 Hwy 707
Murrells Inlet, SC 29576
www.covenantbooks.com

The Most Wonderful Rain

Inspired by a True Story

By
Nermine Khouzam Rubin
and Susan Joy Bellavance
Illustrated by Abdulahi Bonaya Boru

Introduction

The story of Deborah and her African village has a happy ending, but millions of others must trudge each day to find the most basic element of life: Water to drink. But even when that precious water is found, too often, the water is contaminated and it is the cause of misery for those who drink it. For those people, what we take for granted—drinkable water—is part of a daily struggle.

Thanks to Water 4 Mercy, an extraordinary not-for-profit organization, there will be many more Deborahs and many more happy endings. Water 4 Mercy was started by a visionary, courageous, unstoppable woman, Nermine Khouzam Rubin. Inspired by her religious faith that sees all people as her sisters and brothers, Nermine is determined to change the world, one village at a time, and one drinking water well at a time. Yet, even if Nermine and the friends she has inspired to follow her in her mission fail to transform the entire world, it is already true that she has transformed the future of those in every community where her good works are found.

When young women—and it is almost always women!—no longer have to spend the day fetching water for food preparation, bathing, and sanitation, they will no longer be too exhausted to spend what time they have left in their day to learn in school. Or for those a bit older, for those adult women no longer spending the day carrying water, they will have more leisure time to guard their health, and also to learn new skills to bring new prosperity to their villages and their extended families. In this way, Nermine and Water 4 Mercy are doing far more than providing water. They are also providing a future, with many stumbling blocks removed.

May Nermine's tireless energy never flag. There is a big world out there that needs her!

Seth M. Siegel, author of the New York Times bestseller,
***Let There Be Water: Israel's Solution
for a Water-Starved World***

Dedication

Dedication: Nermine Khouzam Rubin, Founder and CEO of Water 4 Mercy

"The Most Wonderful Rain" was produced by my foundation, **Water 4 Mercy**, to touch more hearts to act. I want to reveal to the world the great need of those who suffer from the lack of clean water and to illustrate what happens when caring hearts are awakened and determined to relieve the misery of their brothers and sisters.

To that end, I would like to dedicate this book to God, who touched my heart to bring His life-giving waters, which provide food and hope to thousands of people, thanks to the generosity of our donors.

I thank my co-author Susan Bellavance for her collaboration and support throughout the writing and illustrative process.

I am grateful to the Water 4 Mercy team: Innovation Africa, CultivAid, Don Bosco Technical Institutes, the many organizations, supporters and volunteers whose commitment to serving others reminds us of the power of compassion and generosity. Above all, I thank God, who continues to bless us with the gift of life, and I am grateful to my family who have always been my source of strength and inspiration.

I pray this book will inspire readers to take action and to help make a difference in the lives of others.

Dedication: Susan Joy Bellavance (Author)

To my dear husband, Dale, for his quiet, hidden, loving support in all that I do.

In a tiny village in Tanzania, a rooster crows before dawn.

"Aigh!" groans Deborah from her thin mat on the dirt floor. "Can't I sleep a little more?" But the rooster only crows again.

3

Deborah sits up in the darkness and whispers the words that keep her dearest dream alive: "One day I will be a doctor for my village and for all the region."

But how will her dream ever come true? She aches in her heart to return to school, even for just a day, but it is the dry season. There is no water. Grandmother is too old to carry the heavy buckets any longer. No, there will be no school again today.

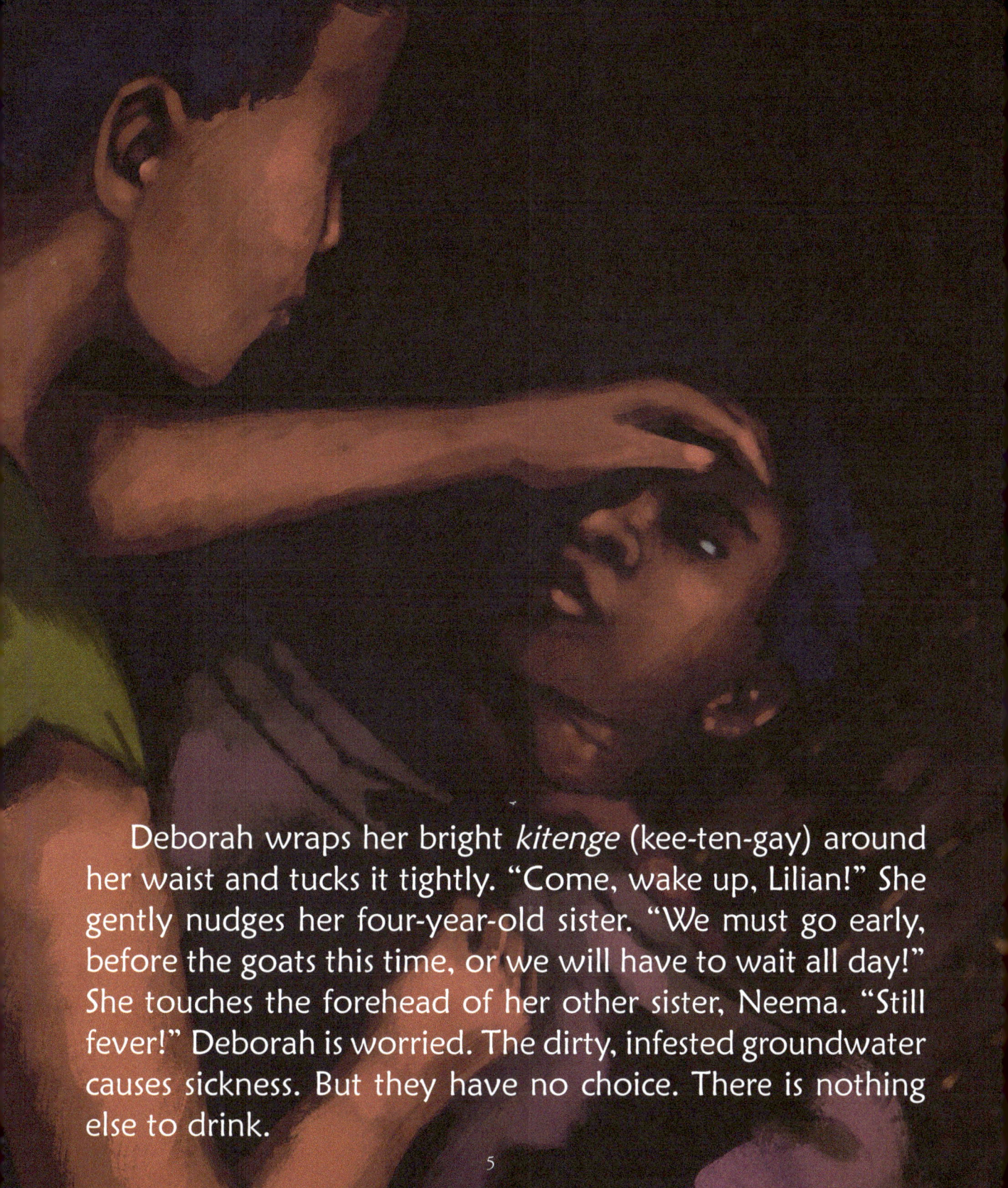

Deborah wraps her bright *kitenge* (kee-ten-gay) around her waist and tucks it tightly. "Come, wake up, Lilian!" She gently nudges her four-year-old sister. "We must go early, before the goats this time, or we will have to wait all day!" She touches the forehead of her other sister, Neema. "Still fever!" Deborah is worried. The dirty, infested groundwater causes sickness. But they have no choice. There is nothing else to drink.

Near the wall of the round, thatched mud hut, Grandmother is snoring softly. A few years ago, Deborah's mother died of typhus from contaminated water. Grandmother cared for the girls. Now, at fourteen, it is Deborah who cares for Grandmother.

"We are going now, Grandmother."

"You should be going to school! Please, God, that you will be safe! If only…"

"Don't worry! We will be careful."

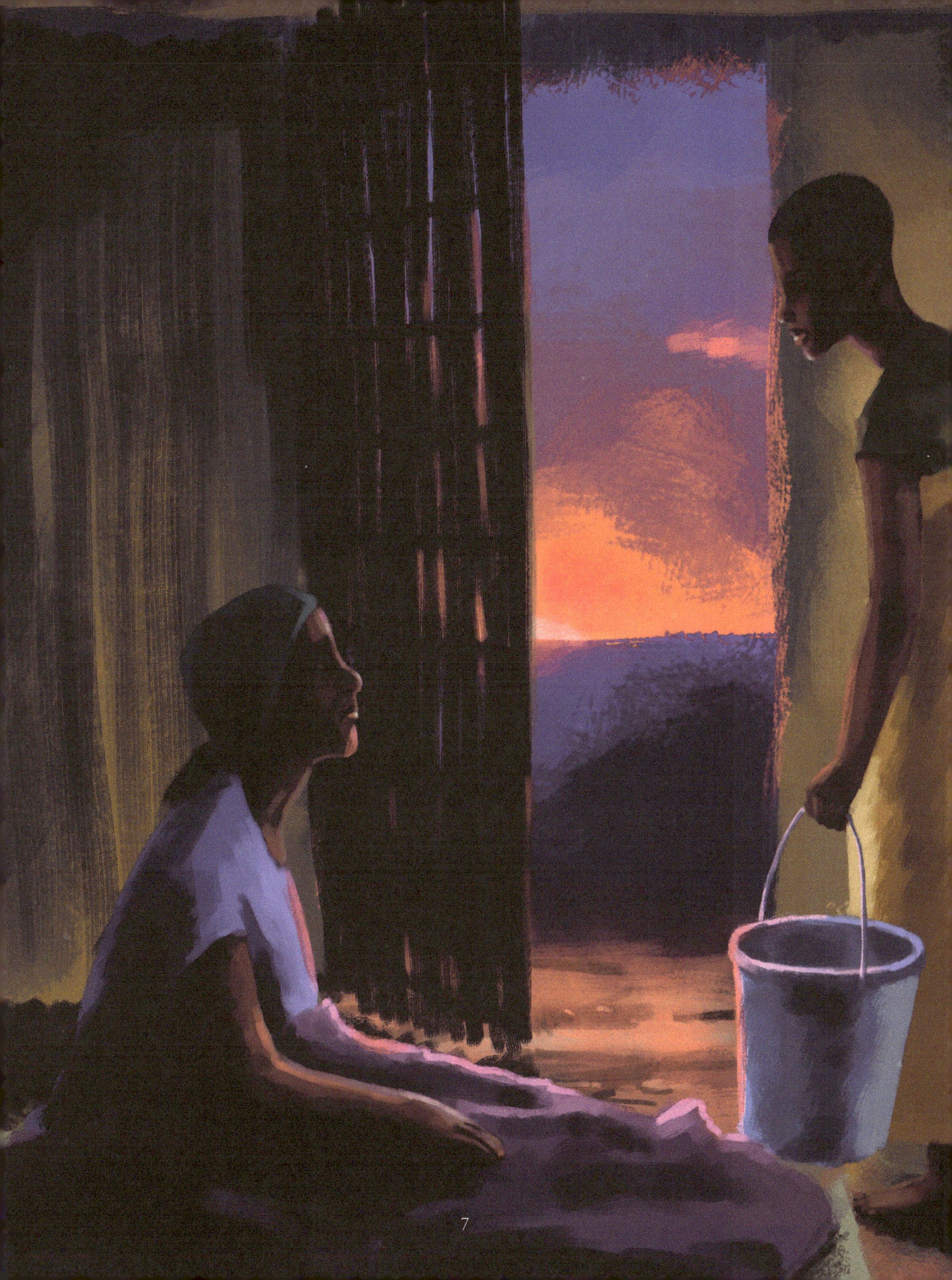

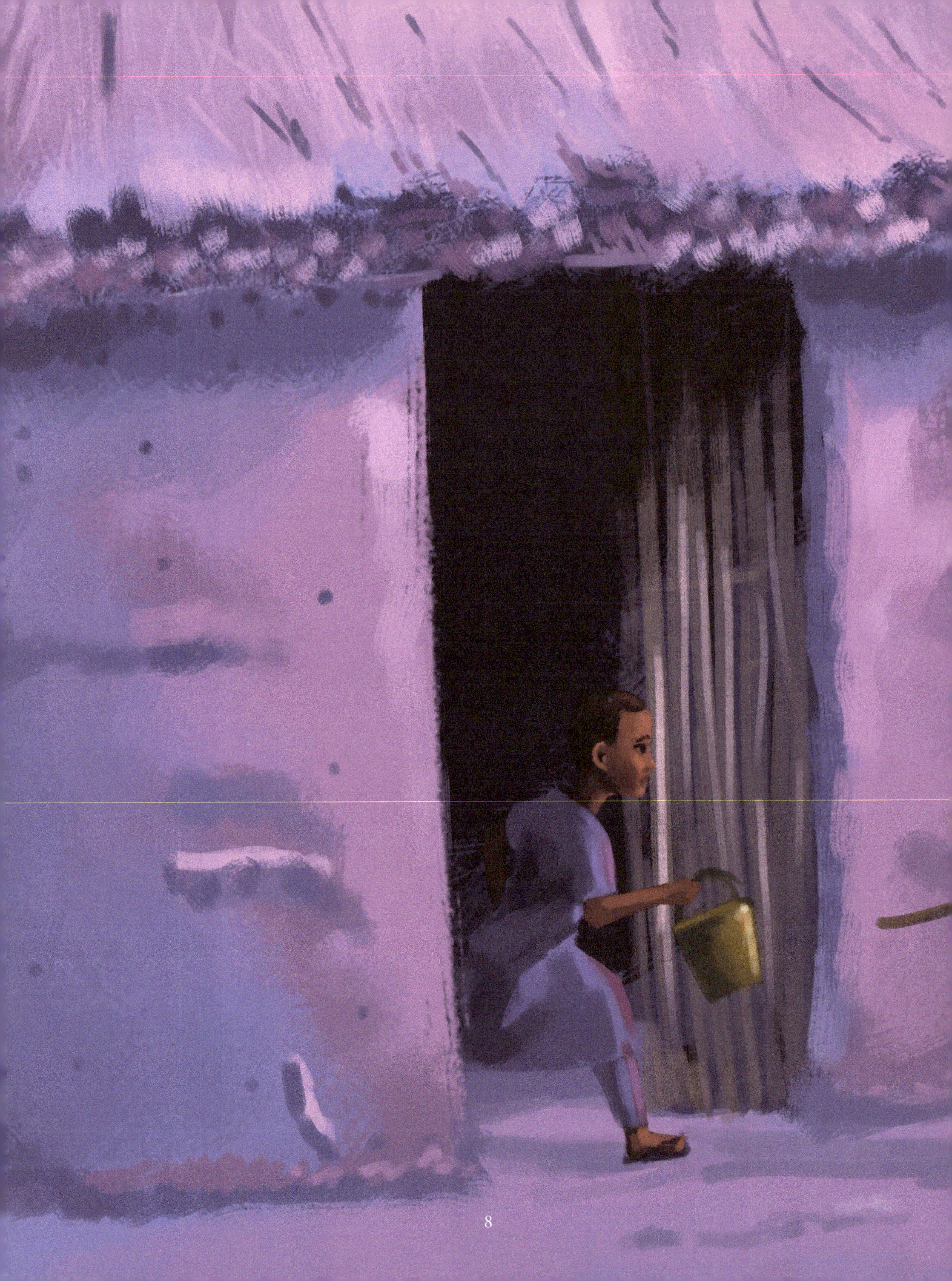

Deborah grabs buckets and her walking stick and pushes open the rickety stick door. Lilian takes the smaller bucket and runs along at Deborah's side trying to keep up. Nervously, they scan the pathway for poisonous snakes. At 4:00 a.m., it is still completely dark.

Deborah squeezes Lilian's shoulder. She doesn't want Lilian to know she is afraid. It takes hours of walking through the bush to get to the public water hole. Anything could happen to them along the way.

Deborah's eyes dart about as they cut across grassy fields dotted with black leafless trees. She is constantly watching for danger—a vicious hyena or worse. Unexpected sounds keep startling them. Lilian stays very close.

12

After three long hours, they come to the last bend in the rocky path. The dusty ground shows hoofprints and goat pellets everywhere.

"Oh, no!" cries Deborah. "No water! The goats have drunk it all!"

Women and children from other villages are already in line before them. Everyone must wait a long time until the water in the dug-out mudhole bubbles up again, forming a new puddle to scoop from.

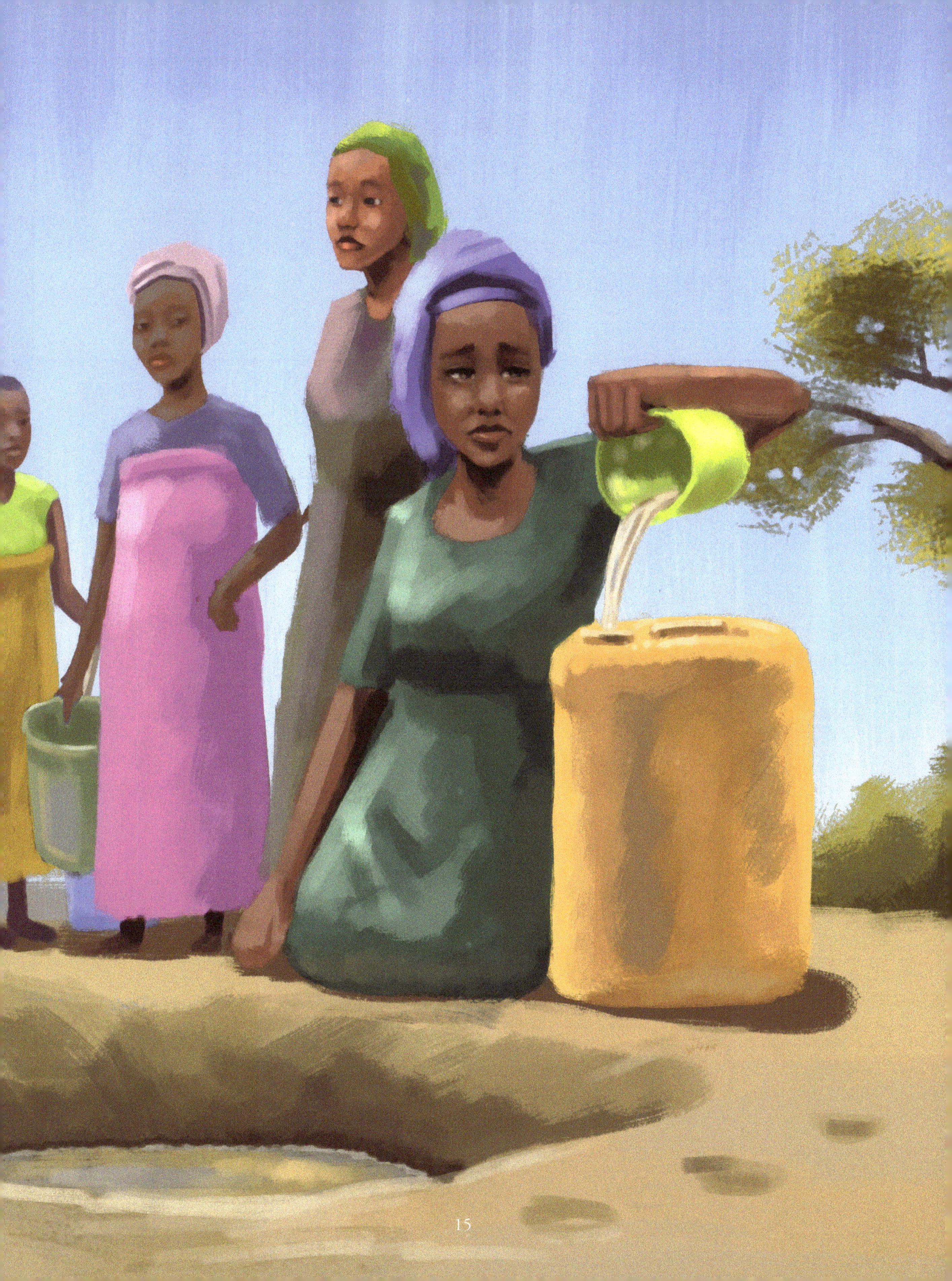

Finally, it is Deborah's turn after three long hours. She scoops the fetid water, trying to brush aside the scum from the top of the puddle. After each scoop, she must wait patiently for more water to slowly seep to the surface. It will take another hour and a half to fill both buckets to the brim.

Finally, Lilian and Deborah take a drink from the last scoop, then step aside for the next person.

Deborah hoists the five-gallon bucket onto her head and starts for home.

Lilian hurries beside her, holding the smaller bucket by the handle. Both are vigilant: they must not waste even one drop of the precious water.

The searing sun makes the long walk home hot and dusty, but it does not slow them down.

Suddenly, the girls hear strangers' voices, and they instinctively scurry off the path. They wait, hidden, still and silent. Deborah's heart beats fast and hard. She clenches her walking stick until the strangers are far in the distance and no longer visible. The girls steal from their hiding place and carefully hurry along the path.

It is ten hours since they left home. Finally, Deborah sees familiar thatched huts. But what is this? The villagers are all gathered around the baobab tree. The chief, the *mwenyekiti*, is speaking. There is a smiling guest standing with him. Her face beams with kindness.

"What can this stranger be about?" Deborah wonders as she draws closer to listen.

"Tomorrow the work crew will come with a drilling machine. Hopefully, by the end of the day, our village will have its own freshwater well!" Everyone cheers except Deborah, who is too stunned to make a sound. Grandmother nears.

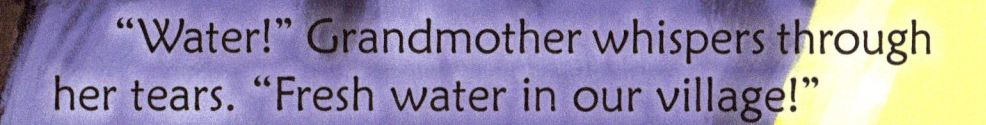

"Water!" Grandmother whispers through her tears. "Fresh water in our village!"

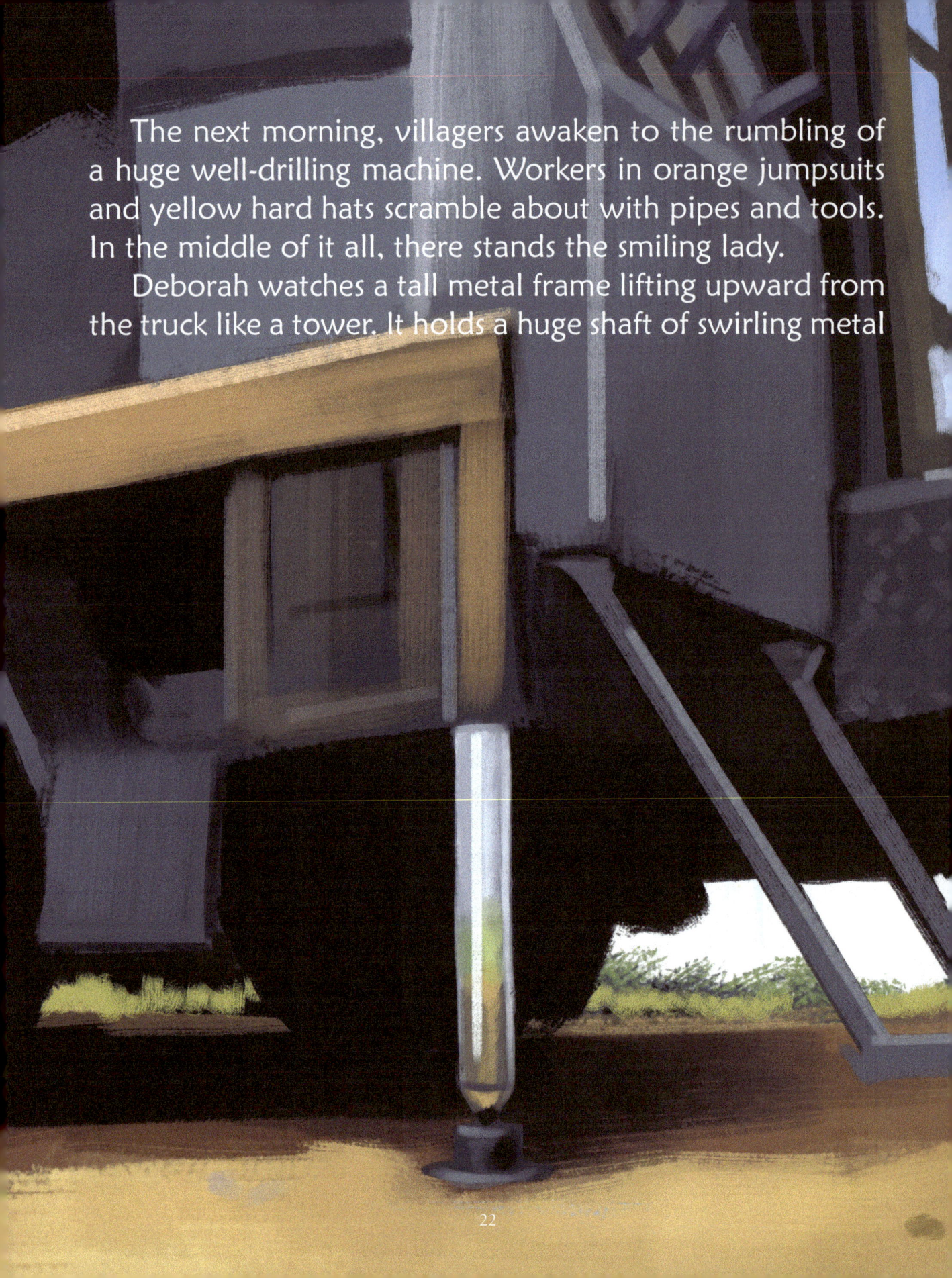

The next morning, villagers awaken to the rumbling of a huge well-drilling machine. Workers in orange jumpsuits and yellow hard hats scramble about with pipes and tools. In the middle of it all, there stands the smiling lady.

Deborah watches a tall metal frame lifting upward from the truck like a tower. It holds a huge shaft of swirling metal that narrows to a sharp point. It is poised like a giant fang ready to strike. The engine growls and roars... The drill bit begins to whirl downward, piercing the hard gray soil. It bites through the earth, searching for water, churning up clods of dirt and rock.

Deborah's heart beats faster. *Water, here? How is that possible?*

Villagers gather around the drilling machine. The crew adds a pipe to the drill bit, then another and another. Deeper and deeper it roils into the ground. Hours and hours pass. The villagers' excitement cools along with the day. Evening approaches. Eventually, the well-digging machine stops. Deborah's heart sinks. *Maybe there is no water beneath my village.*

Early the next morning, Deborah and Lilian reluctantly leave to get water. When they return that afternoon, the machine is roaring again! Deborah's heart sparks with hope. She joins the watching villagers.

Then…a bubbling. Everyone freezes. Could it be?

A trickle streams over the top of the soil mound around the drill. It lightly streams for a long time. Is that it? Then, a sputter! Everyone gasps. All eyes are riveted on the muddy mound.

Suddenly, a huge gush of water bursts into the sky and rains down on everyone!

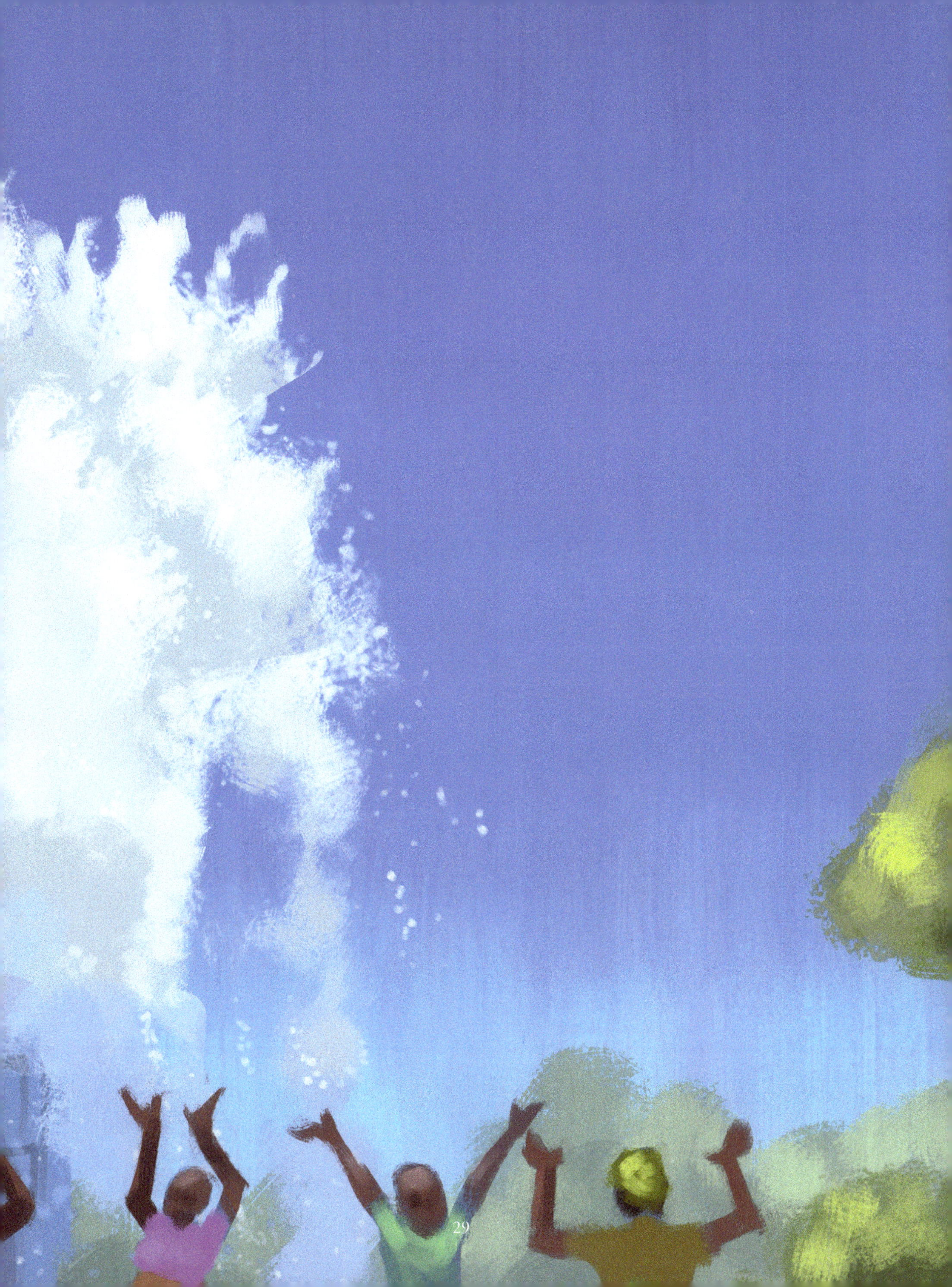

Villagers scream with excitement. There is dancing and praising, singing, laughing, and splashing!

31

Tears of joy mingle with drops of fresh water on Deborah's cheeks. Grandmother rejoices.
It was the most wonderful rain!

In the weeks to come, everyone will pitch in to construct a water tower, lay pipe for water stations, and build water troughs for animals. Hard work that no one will mind!

In a tiny village in Tanzania, a rooster crows before dawn. Deborah reaches for her kitenge to wrap around her body, but it isn't there.

"Wear this," Grandmother says with a smile, handing her a clean school uniform. Deborah washes her face and hands with fresh crystal water.

She steps out of her hut and gazes at the majestic water tower above the village.

"Today my dream lives again. Today I can go to school. Today I can begin again to become a doctor."
Yes, it was the most wonderful rain!

Follow-up questions for *The Most Wonderful Rain*

1. After reading *The Most Wonderful Rain*, how does it make me feel?

2. What would it be like to live day after day without fresh water to drink and use?

3. What is a way that I can help those who do not have clean water?

Need some ideas? Reach out to us! info@water4mercy.org

Epilogue

In August 2018, I founded Water 4 Mercy after witnessing the heart-wrenching devastation of drought in Tanzania. The sight of women and children searching for water for more than 10 hours a day, resorting to drinking animal blood, and facing contaminated water broke my heart. The men's look of hopelessness haunted me, and I knew something had to be done.

Miraculously, I met Seth Siegel, the bestselling author of "Let There Be Water," who inspired me with Israel's proven solutions to water and agricultural crises in Africa. With God's grace, Water 4 Mercy was born, grounded in these winning Israeli principles that incorporate advanced technologies with sustainable practices to break the cycles of poverty and disease, creating 'Bountiful Cycles of Success'.

Water 4 Mercy's projects are 100% successful and remotely monitored live, making our solar-powered water sources resilient against breakdowns and other challenges. Israeli Nongovernmental Organizations, Innovation Africa and CultivAid implement and oversee our water and agricultural projects, respectively. In collaboration with the Don Bosco Technical Institutes of Africa, together we are sharing Israeli knowledge through AITeC, the Agricultural Innovation and Technology Centers. As of 2023, we have transformed the lives of close to 50,000 people and trained over 750 farmers, empowering them to sustain their crops, livestock, and local economies.

Water 4 Mercy is a 501(c)3 nonprofit with a mission "To Uphold Human Dignity by Eradicating Thirst, Hunger, and Poverty" in Africa. If you wish to support us, please visit Water4Mercy.org or send your contributions to 3026 Oakmont Drive, Clearwater, FL 33761, USA.

Together, we are making a difference, one drop at a time.

What is Water 4 Mercy? Water 4 Mercy is:

Water!

Food!

Hope!

Agricultural Innovation and Technology Centers (AITeC)

AITeC - The School of HOPE! Growing A New Generation of Experts for The Future of Food And Nutritional Security.

What makes Water 4 Mercy the most successful organization established to help the suffering people of Africa? Sustainability through education!

Water 4 Mercy founded and funded the Agricultural Innovation and Technology Center (AITeC), incorporating Israel's advanced agricultural knowledge into the existing Don Bosco Technical Institute's hands-on vocational curriculum. At AITeC, students are taught innovative development in the areas of nutrition training, climate resilience, income generation, teacher training, and youth empowerment. Students, alongside local farmers, and extension workers, learn the best sustainable practices in horticulture and animal husbandry from world renowned skilled agronomists and how to improve their undernourished communities' health by "eating the rainbow", a term conveying the consumption of colorful foods for optimal nutritious value. For more information visit https://aitecfarm.com/.

With Dom Bosco Technical Institutes spanning the continent, Water 4 Mercy sees endless opportunities to bring water and agricultural technology all over Africa! At AITeC, students are taught innovative development in the areas of nutrition training, climate resilience, income generation, teacher training, and youth empowerment.

Students, alongside local farmers, and extension workers, learn the best sustainable practices in horticulture and animal husbandry from world renowned skilled agronomists and how to improve their undernourished communities' health by "eating the rainbow", a term conveying the consumption of colorful foods for optimal nutritious value.

About the Illustrator

Abdulahi Bonaya Boru, Artist Illustrator

Abdulahi Bonaya Boru

Abdulahi Bonaya Boru resides in Gotu Village, Isiolo County, Kenya. Ancestrally from the Borana Tribe, a nomadic community of pastoralists, young Abdulahi discovered his passion for art using readily available charcoal to capture the landscape and culture of his village. Art has become his lifelong passion.

Abdulahi also works as a communications officer in Isiolo Peace Link, a civil organization in Isiolo, Kenya which addresses civic laws, climate change, and human rights. Abdulahi is a member of Artvista, using art to shape and effect community issues.

Abdulahi hopes to assemble a home studio that is digital and traditional so that he can create art locally in Isiolo to share internationally. A youth leader who teaches art classes locally, Abdulahi dreams of creating an art school in his village, inspiring students with skills that open them up to the world.

About the Authors

Nermine Khouzam Rubin, MBA, MHS, Founder & CEO, Water 4 Mercy

Nermine immigrated from Egypt at 8 years old after she, her parents, and 4 siblings lived through the 6-Day Arab-Israeli War in Port Said. In 2018 she founded Water 4 Mercy and contracted with the world's leading experts in solar, water and agriculture to provide a *permanent solution* for breaking the vicious cycles of poverty *in Africa*. She is the visionary of AITeC, the Agricultural Innovation and Technology Center, designed to transfer agricultural knowledge by combining Israeli expertise with the premier vocational education of Catholic Don Bosco Technical Institutes of Africa.

Nermine resides in Clearwater, Florida with her husband Leslie of 31+ years, and has 2 adult children, Samantha, and Nathan.

Susan Joy Bellavance, Author

Susan Joy Bellavance served with the Missionaries of Charity, later becoming a Parochial school teacher and a founding member of Mount Royal Academy. She has served as a catechist, youth formator and a long-term volunteer at Bishop Peterson Residence for retired priests. Susan and husband Dale reside in Newbury, New Hampshire have two married daughters, Sophia (son in law Jonathan), and Marguerite (son in law David), and 2 grandchildren Evelyn and Augustine.

Susan's other published works include: In My Mother's Womb, King of the Shattered Glass, Will You Come to Mass? The Light of Christmas Morning, and When Jesus Speaks.